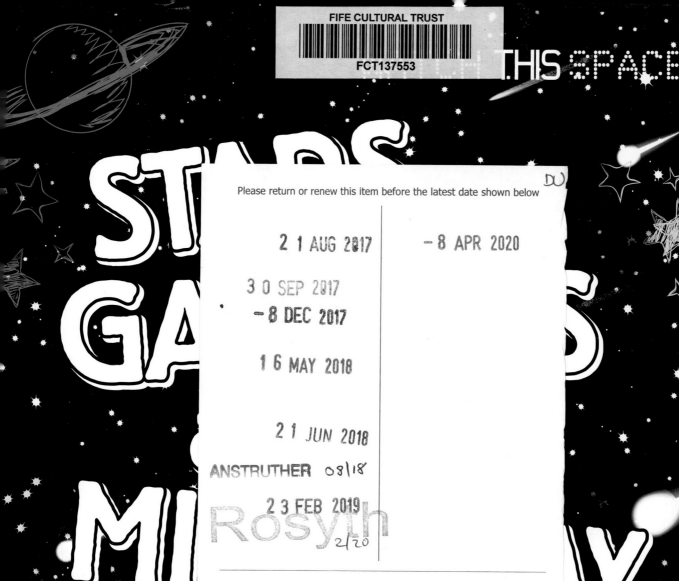

Published in paperback in 2016
First published in hardback in 2015
© Wayland 2015

Wayland
An imprint of
Hachette Children's Group
Part of Hodder & Stoughton
Carmelite House
50 Victoria Embankment
London EC4Y 0DZ

Editor: Izzi Howell
Designer: Clare Nicholas
Cover design and concept: Lisa Peacock

A catalogue for this title is available from the British Library

ISBN: 978 0 7502 9227 6
Library eBook ISBN: 978 0 7502 9226 9
Dewey Number: 523.8-dc23

10 9 8 7 6 5 4 3
Printed in China

Produced by White-Thomson Publishing Ltd.

White-Thomson Publishing Ltd
www.wtpub.co.uk
+44 (0) 843 208 7460

MIX
Paper from
responsible sources
FSC® C104740
FSC
www.fsc.org

Wayland, part of Hachette Children's Group and published by Hodder and Stoughton Limited

www.hachette.co.uk

The website addresses (URLs) included in this book were valid at the time of going to press. However, because of the nature of the Internet, it is possible that some addresses may have changed, or sites may have changed or closed down since publication. While the author and publisher regret any inconvenience this may cause the readers, no responsibility for any such changes can be accepted by either the author or the publisher.

Picture credits
Shutterstock/A-R-T cover (background), Shutterstock/notkoo cover (tl), Dreamstime/Goinyk Volodymyr cover (tc), NASA, Jeff Hester, and Paul Scowen (Arizona State University) cover (bl), Shutterstock/Petrafler cover (bl), Shutterstock/Vadim Sadovski cover (br), Shutterstock/A-R-T title page (background), Shutterstock/solarseven title page (bc).

Shutterstock/vit-plus 4 (background), Shutterstock/Lorelyn Medina 4 (bl), Shutterstock/fad82 4 (bl), ESA/NASA/Hubble 4 (br), NASA/JPL-Caltech 5 (tr), Shutterstock/RedKoala 5 (br), Shutterstock/RedKoala 6 (bl), Science Photo Library/Lionel Bret/Look At Sciences 7, Shutterstock/Catmando 8 (l), Shutterstock/andromina 8 (bc), Stefan Chabluk 9, Science Photo Library/Mark Garlick 10 (tl), Shutterstock/Happy Art 10 (bl), Shutterstock/gornjak 11 (bl), ESA/Hubble & NASA 11 (tr), NASA, ESA, and JPL-Caltech 11 (br), NASA/Penn State University 12 (tl), NASA/CXC/JPL-Caltech/STScI 12 (bl), ESA/Akira Fujii 13, NASA/Rogelio Bernal Andreo (Deep Sky Colors) 14 (tr), Science Photo Library/Christian Darkin 14 (bc), Shutterstock/bioraven 15 (tr), Wikimedia/Sephirohq 15 (br), Wikimedia/Antonello Zito 16 (bl), NASA/Dana Berry, Sky Works Digital 16 (tr), Thinkstock/lilipom 17 (bl), NASA/ESA/Hubble Heritage (STScI/AURA)-Hubble/Europe Collab. 17 (tr), Shutterstock/bioraven 17 (br), Shutterstock/sciencepics 18-19, ESO 20-21 (c), Shutterstock/Skocko 21 (tr), Shutterstock/Lorelyn Medina 21 (br), NASA/Dana Berry 22 (tl), Shutterstock/RainsGraphics 22 (bl), Shutterstock/vector illustration 23 (bl), Wikimedia/Mysid/Jm smits 23 (tr), X-ray: NASA/CXC/SAO; Optical: Detlef Hartmann; Infrared: NASA/JPL-Caltech 24, NASA/JPL-Caltech/STScI/Vassar 25 (bc), Shutterstock/Malinovskaya Yulia 25 (tr), X-ray - NASA / CXC / Caltech / P.Ogle et al., Optical - NASA/STScI, IR - NASA/JPL-Caltech, Radio - NSF/NRAO/VLA 26 (bl), Shutterstock/RedKoala 26 (br), NASA/JPL-Caltech 27, NASA/ JPL 28, Shutterstock/Viktar Malyshchyts 29 (tc), Shutterstock/fattoboi83 29 (tr), Shutterstock/andromina 29 (br).

Design elements throughout: Shutterstock/PinkPueblo, Shutterstock/topform, Shutterstock/Nikiteev_Konstantin, Shutterstock/Vadim Sadovski, Shutterstock/CPdesign, Shutterstock/Elinalee, Shutterstock/Hilch.

CONTENTS

STARRY SKIES

Distant stars and planets both look like small pinpricks of light, but they are quite different bodies. Planets shine in the night sky because their surfaces reflect light from another source. Stars are the real deal: they shine by producing their own light.

What Is A Star?

A star is a massive sphere of gas, bound together by gravity. Stars give off large amounts of heat and light energy. This energy is generated in the core of the star.

FAMILIES OF STARS

Galaxies are enormous collections of stars, planets and clouds of dust and gas, all kept together by gravity – the force of attraction between objects. Our galaxy is called the Milky Way. Its galactic neighbours include the Large Magellanic Cloud and the mighty Andromeda Galaxy.

Twinkle, twinkle, little star, how I wonder what you are?

Well, it's a giant ball of gas, mostly hydrogen, held together by its own gravity.

the Large Magellanic Cloud

Long Light

The distances in space are MASSIVE, far too large to measure in kilometres, so astronomers measure in light years. A light year is the distance light travels in an entire year. Bearing in mind that light covers a whopping 299,792,458 metres in a single second, a light year is a long, long way – 9,460,528,404,847 km.

HELLO NEIGHBOURS!

The Canis Major Dwarf is one of the closest galaxies to Earth – only 25,000 light years away. The Andromeda Galaxy is also thought of as a neighbour, yet it is over two million light years away.

the stunning Andromeda Galaxy

HOW MANY STARS ARE THERE?

No one is totally sure. The European Space Agency estimates that there are at least one hundred billion stars in the Milky Way alone. Multiply that by the number of other galaxies in the universe and you get an unbelievably HUGE number.

4.24

THE DISTANCE IN LIGHT YEARS FROM EARTH TO PROXIMA CENTAURI, THE NEAREST STAR OUTSIDE OUR SOLAR SYSTEM.

OUR NEAREST STAR

Big enough to fit 103 million Earths inside it, the Sun is a mere 149.6 million km from our planet. That may sound like a huge distance to us, but it's close enough for astronomers to study it in detail.

CORE, BLIMEY!

The high pressure and temperature in the Sun's core cause the nuclei of hydrogen atoms to join together to form helium. This process is called nuclear fusion. It generates vast amounts of heat and light energy.

LONG JOURNEY

Energy from the core travels in waves through the Sun's radiative zone – a journey that may take as long as 100,000 years. This energy then moves through the convection zone, on swirling currents of hot gas, before reaching the surface.

100,000

THE HEIGHT IN KILOMETRES OF SOME LARGE SOLAR PROMINENCES, MORE THAN 11,000 TIMES THE HEIGHT OF MOUNT EVEREST.

WHAT IS THE SUN MADE OF?

The Sun is made up of around 74% hydrogen, 25% helium and small amounts of other elements.

The Sun's outer atmosphere, or corona, stretches out over several million kilometres. Some parts reach temperatures of 2 million °C.

Rising and falling currents in the convection zone carry energy to the surface.

Solar prominences are large clouds of hot gas that occasionally shoot up from the Sun's surface.

Sunspots are part of the Sun's surface that appear darker because they are cooler than the surrounding areas.

Inside the Sun

The dense radiative zone surrounds the core.

The core of the Sun is phenomenally hot – around 15 million °C.

The Sun's surface, or photosphere, is made of hot gases, with an average temperature of 5,500 °C.

Above the photosphere is the chromosphere – the Sun's 2,000-km-thick inner atmosphere.

A PROTOSTAR IS BORN

Pillars of Creation

Stars are born in giant clouds called stellar nebulae. These provide us with some of the most breathtaking sights found in the universe. Recently-formed stars are known as protostars.

Clouding Around

Stellar nebulae are formed of gas and dust. These clouds can be far larger than our entire solar system, which is 1–3 light years wide. The Thor's Helmet Nebula measures over 30 light years across.

EAGLE EYES

The Eagle Nebula is around 6,000 light years from Earth. Spectacular images of it have been captured by the Hubble Space Telescope. Within the nebula, there are columns of gas and dust reaching an astounding 37 trillion km high. Astronomers call these the 'Pillars of Creation'.

800,000

THE ESTIMATED NUMBER OF STARS AND PROTOSTARS FOUND IN THE TARANTULA NEBULA.

The Start Of A Star

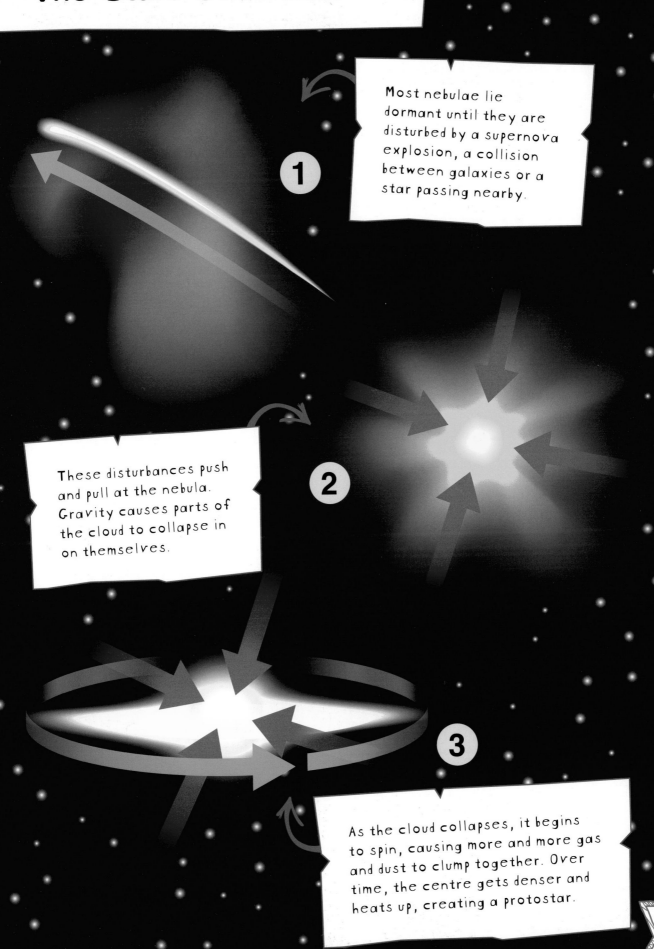

1 Most nebulae lie dormant until they are disturbed by a supernova explosion, a collision between galaxies or a star passing nearby.

2 These disturbances push and pull at the nebula. Gravity causes parts of the cloud to collapse in on themselves.

3 As the cloud collapses, it begins to spin, causing more and more gas and dust to clump together. Over time, the centre gets denser and heats up, creating a protostar.

MAIN SEQUENCE STARS

As a protostar grows, its core becomes denser and hotter. At around 10 million °C, a protostar's core may ignite and start turning hydrogen into helium, generating monstrous amounts of energy as a result.

Hydrogen is converted to helium in a nuclear fusion reaction.

In Sequence

Once a star is carrying out nuclear fusion, it is said to be in its main sequence. Most stars spend the majority of their life as a main sequence star, only changing when they run out of hydrogen as fuel. The Sun is roughly halfway through its main sequence, which will last 9–10 billion years. Most of the stars we can observe in space are in their main sequence.

36 BILLION
THE APPROXIMATE AMOUNT OF HYDROGEN, IN TONNES, THAT THE SUN USES AS FUEL IN ITS NUCLEAR REACTIONS EVERY MINUTE. DON'T WORRY — IT HAS ENOUGH TO CONTINUE TO BURN BRIGHTLY FOR MANY BILLIONS OF YEARS.

Pressure vs. Gravity

Two competing forces, pressure and gravity, stop main sequence stars from changing shape or size. Gravity pulls gas in towards the centre of the star, while pressure from the star's core pushes outwards.

Proxima Centauri is a main sequence star. Although it is the nearest star to our solar system, it is not visible to the naked eye because it isn't very bright.

FAILED STARS

Smaller protostars, with less than a tenth of the Sun's mass, never become real stars. They don't have enough mass to carry out nuclear fusion, so they exist as warm bodies in space called brown dwarfs. They tend to be between 10 and 80 times the size of Jupiter.

Discovered in 2014, WISE 0855–0714 is the coolest known brown dwarf with a temperature of -48 to -13 °C. Chilly!

an artist's impression of a brown dwarf

SEEING STARS

Up to 6,000 stars can be seen from Earth with the naked eye. Telescopes and other instruments have revealed many millions more.

WISE 0855-0714

6 LIGHT YEARS

WISE 1049-5319

Barnard's Star

4 LIGHT YEARS

Alpha Centauri

Proxima Centauri

2 LIGHT YEARS

Sun

Super-Close Stars

About a dozen stars are less than 10 light years away from us. Further out, the number of stars increases. Between 10 and 50 light years away, there are 2,000 known stars.

Stars 'twinkling' in the Small Magellanic Cloud.

WHY DO STARS TWINKLE?

Actually, most stars don't twinkle. It is Earth's moving atmosphere that causes the light from a star to bend, giving the impression of flickering.

Travelling In Time

Powerful telescopes can peer deep into the night sky and spot dimmer and more distant stars. The further away a star is, the longer it takes for its light to travel through space to reach Earth. This means that if astronomers view a star 1,000 light years away, they are actually viewing what it looked like 1,000 years ago. Awesome!

SEEING FAR

Some stars can be seen clearly in the night sky despite being extremely distant. Rho Cassiopeiae is a giant star around 8,200 light years from Earth. Yet, because it shines much more brightly than the Sun, it can be viewed from the northern hemisphere of Earth without a telescope.

APPARENTLY...

Apparent magnitude is a measure of how bright a star is when viewed from Earth. The lower the magnitude, the brighter the star. The brightest star from Earth is the Sun, at -26.74 magnitude, followed by Sirius, at -1.46 magnitude.

the night sky

Procyon
(magn. 0.38)

Betelgeuse
(magn. 0.5)

Sirius
(magn. -1.46)

STAR QUALITY

Not all stars look the same. Stars vary greatly in size, colour, temperature and brightness.

Hot Stuff!

The Sun is far from the hottest star around. Some stars have a surface temperature over six times hotter than the Sun. Delta Circini, for instance, is a star with a surface temperature of around 35,000 °C. What a scorcher!

Rigel, a star with a whopping 100-million-km diameter, casts its blue-white light over the Witch Head Nebula.

Witch Head Nebula

SPECTRAL TYPES

Astronomers group stars into classes, called spectral types, based on their colour and temperature. There are seven main types. The Sun is a type G star.

Spectral Type	Colour	Temperature °C	Star Examples
O	Blue	>30,000	Delta Circini, Sigma Orionis
B	Blue-white	9,750–30,000	Z Canis Majoris, Rigel
A	White	7,100–9,750	Sirius A, Vega, Fomalhaut B
F	Yellow-white	5,900–7,100	Canopus, Wasp-24
G	Yellowish	5,200–5,900	The Sun, Alpha Centauri
K	Orange	3,900–5,200	Pollux, Gliese 86, Arcturus
M	Reddish	2,000–3,900	Antares, Proxima Centauri

O   B   A   F   G   K   M

RED DWARFS

The smallest stars that fuse hydrogen are known as red dwarfs. More than half of the stars in the universe may be red dwarfs, including our nearest star, Proxima Centauri. As a result, they may last a thousand billion years before their hydrogen is used up. They will then collapse inwards under their own weight and become black dwarfs.

20
THE NUMBER OF SECONDS IT TAKES THE PISTOL STAR, A SPECTRAL TYPE B STAR, TO GIVE OFF THE SAME AMOUNT OF ENERGY AS THE SUN DOES IN A YEAR.

Mu Cephei was nicknamed the 'Garnet Star' for its deep red colour. It is one of the most luminous stars, around 350,000 times brighter than the Sun.

Bright Lights

Luminosity is a measure of how much energy a star gives off. You can think of it as how brightly a star shines. A star that shines more brightly than others in the night sky is either closer to us or has greater luminosity than the others. Rigel is over 800 light years away, but it is the seventh brightest star viewable from Earth because of its intense luminosity – 117,000 times stronger than the Sun's.

STRANGE STARS

Some stars hang around in pairs, steal gas and dust from other stars or vary how brightly they shine. Meet some of the strangest stars in space.

Paired Up

Binary stars are pairs of stars that are bound together by their mutual gravity. The two stars orbit the centre point of their mass. The star Sirius, perceived by the naked eye as one single star, is actually a binary star pair, made up of Sirius A and B.

These two white-dwarf binary stars are locked in an orbit that shrinks by 2.5 cm per hour. Scientists estimate that they will merge in a few hundred thousand years.

STELLAR STEAL

Some binary stars interact with each other. One star 'steals' matter from the other star. The matter either makes the star swell in size or forms a disc, called an accretion disc, around the star.

Stolen matter from the larger star is forming an accretion disc around the smaller star.

accretion disc

On And Off

Cepheid variable stars change their brightness over regular periods — six weeks in the case of RS Puppis. The fluctuation of light caused by the swelling and shrinking of this variable star helped scientists to accurately calculate the star as being 6,500 light years from Earth, with a 1% margin of error.

RS Puppis is 200 times larger and 15,000 times brighter than the Sun.

STAR SYSTEMS

Some stars aren't just part of a pair, they are part of a star system containing three, four or more stars all bound together by gravity. Algol, for example, is a star system made up of three stars. Every 68 hours, the orbits in which two of these stars move causes one to eclipse the other, blocking it out when viewed from Earth.

100–1,000

THE NUMBER OF SECONDS IT TAKES ZZ CETI VARIABLE STARS TO CHANGE BRIGHTNESS. THAT'S FAST!

Off You Go!

The force of gravity between the four stars in the T Tauri star system has recently caused its smallest member, about a fifth of the size of the Sun, to be flung out of the system!

STAR DEATH

Stars don't exist forever. When a star runs out of hydrogen to fuel its nuclear fusion reactions, it is said to end its main sequence. The size and mass of a star will determine what happens to it in its final stages.

RED GIANTS

If a star is around the size of the Sun, it will continue to carry out nuclear fusion with the hydrogen from its outer layers. This causes its core to shrink and its outer layers to expand. The star swells in size, becoming a red giant.

SUPERGIANTS

If a star is much bigger than the Sun, it will follow the same process to become a red giant, continuing to grow until it becomes a red supergiant.

Sun-sized star

massive star

COLOURFUL CLOUDS

As the red giant runs out of fuel, its core collapses. The star's outer layers are flung away, creating clouds called planetary nebula.

WHITE DWARFS

When the planetary nebula disperses, the core of the former red dwarf remains as a white dwarf. White dwarfs are small, dense bodies that cool over time.

white dwarf

red giant

planetary nebula

Type II supernova

red supergiant

neutron star

EXPLOSIVE END

When a supergiant runs out of fuel, it explodes as a Type II supernova. It will go on to become a neutron star or a black hole.

black hole

SUPERNOVA!

Supernovae are giant explosions that rip a star apart. These star deaths are among the most violent events that happen anywhere in the universe.

Types Ia And II

Supernovae occur in different ways. A Type Ia supernova occurs when matter is transferred between two binary stars. A Type II supernova occurs when a large star runs out of hydrogen fuel, swells to become a supergiant and starts fusing heavier and heavier elements in its core. Eventually, the core cannot support its own mass and starts collapsing in on itself rapidly.

EXPLOSIVE EVENTS

As the star's core collapses dramatically, energy causes an ENORMOUS shock wave to rebound outwards, blowing away the outer layers of the star with tremendous force and speed. Astronomers measured debris from the 1987A supernova and found it hurtling away at speeds of 30 million km/h!

HOW HOT IS A SUPERNOVA?

The surface of a supernova may reach 200,000 °C, but at its core, temperatures may soar as high as 100 billion °C. This creates vast amounts of light energy. Some supernovae may shine more brightly than an entire galaxy.

Scientists imagine that a Type Ia supernova looks something like this.

Daytime Viewing

The last major supernova in the Milky Way seen from Earth was Kepler's Supernova, named after the famous German astronomer Johannes Kepler. He was able to view it in 1604 with the naked eye even though it was located 20,000 light years away. This supernova was so bright that for three weeks it could be seen during the day from Earth.

10 BILLION
THE NUMBER OF TIMES BRIGHTER THAN THE SUN THAT A SUPERNOVA MAY SHINE AS IT EXPLODES.

ANCIENT REMAINS

The remains of a supernova can provide long-lasting viewing for astronomers. In 1054 CE, Chinese astronomers spotted a star in the night sky that was bright enough to be observed for the following two years. Scientists believe this was a giant supernova whose remains formed the Crab Nebula, which is studied by astronomers to this day.

Young Guns

In 2011, 10-year-old Canadian schoolgirl Kathryn Aurora Gray discovered a new supernova, Supernova 2010lt, while studying photos taken by a powerful telescope at Abbey Ridge in Canada. Two years later, her brother Nathan also discovered a new supernova!

NEUTRON STARS AND PULSARS

A supernova scatters most of a star's material across space, but a small, very heavy core can remain, collapsing in on itself even further to reduce its atoms to neutrons and form a neutron star.

Incredibly Dense

Neutron stars are the densest stars of all. Most measure around 20 km in diameter yet contain as much matter as the entire solar system. To put it another way, if you could ever grab a spoonful of neutron star, it would crush the spoon immediately, as it would weigh more than a million tonnes.

Astronomers have discovered around 2,000 neutron stars in space so far.

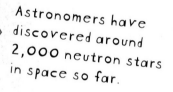

Heavy Stuff
According to scientists, a lump of neutron star the size of a cricket ball would weigh 20 billion tonnes – around 40 times the weight of all the people on Earth!

A MATTER OF SOME GRAVITY

Neutron stars are too small to create light by nuclear fusion, but their great mass means they exert an incredible amount of gravity. The gravity you would experience on a particularly dense neutron star could be as much as a trillion times what we experience on Earth.

In A Spin

Discovered in 1967, pulsars are neutron stars that spin and send out regular streams of matter and radiation. The Vela pulsar completes 11 spins every second, faster than helicopter blades. It also emits a jet of matter that is almost three-quarters of a light year long.

The pulsar spins on its axis.

jets of matter

pulsar

matter and radiation

axis

BURSTING WITH ENERGY

A neutron star's intense gravity puts its surface under huge pressure. Sometimes, parts of the surface break, releasing a giant burst of energy called a starquake. One starquake recorded in 2004 lasted just a fraction of a second, but it released an estimated 10,000 trillion trillion trillion watts of energy. Wow!

43,000
THE NUMBER OF COMPLETE SPINS THE FASTEST KNOWN PULSAR, J1748-2446AD, MAKES EVERY MINUTE.

WHAT IS A MAGNETAR?

A magnetar is a neutron star with an incredibly powerful magnetic field, approximately one thousand times stronger than that of an ordinary neutron star, and hundreds of millions of times stronger than any man-made magnet.

GALAXIES

Galaxies are giant groupings of stars, planets, nebulae, interstellar matter (clouds of gas and dust) and other bodies, held together by gravity.

Number Of Stars

The number of stars in a galaxy varies greatly. A small galaxy contains fewer than one billion stars, but some galaxies hold over 400 billion stars. The Andromeda Galaxy is thought to contain as many as a trillion stars!

WHY DO MANY GALAXY NAMES START WITH THE LETTER 'M'?

The M stands for Messier Catalogue, a list of galaxies and nebulae put together by the French astronomer Charles Messier and his assistant, Pierre Méchain, in the 18th century.

Astronomers have found over 3,000 regions of the M101 galaxy (also known as the Pinwheel Galaxy) in which new stars are being formed. M101 is about 170,000 light years wide.

Crash, Bang, Wallop!

Galaxies occasionally collide with one another. These collisions can continue for millions of years. The two colliding Antennae galaxies have been crashing into each other for at least 100 million years. The massive forces created by the collision are helping to trigger the formation of new stars.

103

THE NUMBER OF OBJECTS, INCLUDING MANY GALAXIES, LISTED IN MESSIER'S FINAL CATALOGUE, PUBLISHED IN THE 1780s. ALL MESSIER OBJECTS CAN BE SPOTTED USING A SMALL TELESCOPE OR GOOD BINOCULARS.

LONG CRUNCH

Another pair of galaxies, NGC 2207 and IC 2163, have just started colliding. Scientists estimate that it will take a billion years for the two galaxies to merge, forming one giant elliptical galaxy.

Some people think that these colliding galaxies look like a mask.

GALAXY TYPES

Galaxies come in many different shapes and sizes. These shapes include elliptical, spiral, barred spiral, lenticular and irregular.

Old Ovals

Elliptical galaxies have a round or oval shape and tend to contain more old stars and fewer new stars than some other types of galaxy. Astronomers rate these galaxies on their roundness from E0 for a near-perfect ball to E7 for a long, cigar-shaped oval.

The M106 spiral galaxy is moving away from us at a speed of 537 km/s — that's 1,933,200 km/h!

IN A SPIRAL

Amongst the most majestic-looking of all galaxies, spirals appear to have a series of long curving arms packed full of stars, nebulae and gas when viewed from above or below. Some, like the Sombrero Galaxy, can only be seen side-on from Earth.

5.5 MILLION
THE ESTIMATED DIAMETER IN LIGHT YEARS OF THE BIGGEST KNOWN GALAXY, IC1101.

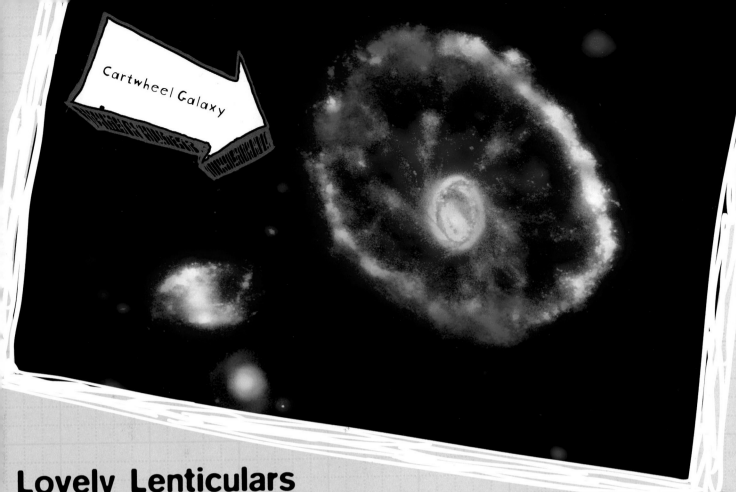

Cartwheel Galaxy

Lovely Lenticulars

These have a bulge in the middle like spiral galaxies, but no swirling arms. The Cartwheel Galaxy is an unusual lenticular galaxy. Astronomers believe it was hit by a smaller galaxy around 100 million years ago, and this caused ripples of intense new star formation, creating a ring around the galaxy's centre.

NOT FITTING IN

Some galaxies don't fit in to any category. These are called irregular galaxies and may have been caused by collisions or near misses with other galaxies, which pulled them out of shape. The Large Magellanic Cloud, a neighbour of the Milky Way, is an irregular galaxy. It is thought to contain around 10 billion stars.

WHAT IS A BARRED SPIRAL GALAXY?

Viewed from space, some spiral galaxies have what looks like a solid bulge or block across their centre, made up of gas, dust and stars. These are known as barred spirals. New stars form at the end of the bar and in the galaxy's arms.

27

THE MILKY WAY

The Milky Way is the galaxy we call home. We cannot view the whole galaxy because we're in it, but scientists have figured out that it is a large barred spiral galaxy made up of a flattish disc of stars, gas and dust, with arms spiralling out from the centre.

Vital Statistics

The solar system may feel like a pretty big place, but light can travel from the Sun past all the planets in less than a day. In contrast, the Milky Way is ENORMOUS! It takes light over 100,000 years to cross the entire Milky Way.

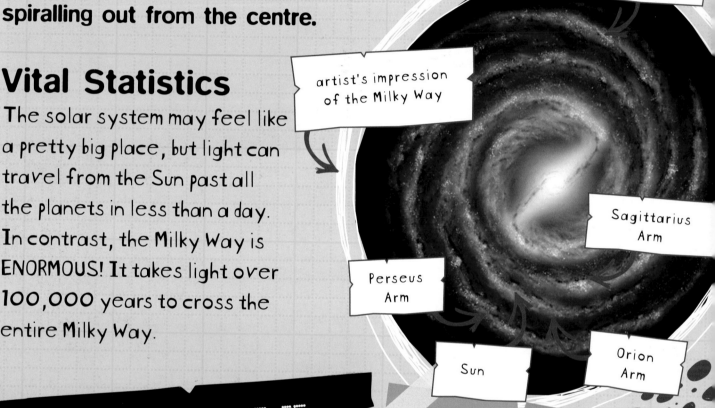

Scutum-Centaurus Arm

artist's impression of the Milky Way

Sagittarius Arm

Perseus Arm

Sun

Orion Arm

WHAT'S IN THE CENTRE OF THE MILKY WAY?

Scientists think there is a supermassive black hole at the heart of our galaxy, which they have named Sagittarius A. Black holes are points in space with so much matter that their gravity is strong enough to pull anything, including light, into it.

LOCATION, LOCATION

The solar system isn't slap bang in the middle of things. We are situated about 27,000 light years from the centre of the Milky Way. We are positioned in between two of the galaxy's main spiral arms – the Perseus and Sagittarius on the Orion arm.

Long-Distance Trip

The solar system orbits the centre of the Milky Way at an extremely rapid speed of 792,000 km/h, but the vast journey it has to make means that a complete orbit takes around 225 million years.

Galaxy Eater

The Milky Way is a cannibal galaxy. In the past, it has consumed small galaxies, drawn in by its gravity, and it is currently gobbling up the Canis Major Dwarf Galaxy.

OLD-TIMER

Around 190 light years from us in the Milky Way is the oldest known star in the entire universe. HD 140283, also known as the Methuselah star, is estimated to be at least 13.2 billion years old, almost as old as the universe itself!

100 BILLION

THE MINIMUM NUMBER OF STARS IN THE MILKY WAY.

GLOSSARY

apparent magnitude – a measurement of how bright a star is when viewed from Earth.

billion – a thousand million.

black hole – an object in space with such strong gravity that nothing nearby can escape its pull, including light.

core – the centre of a star.

density – a measure of how much matter an object contains. If something is very dense, then it contains a lot of matter in a small space.

diameter – the distance across the middle of a circle, or through the middle of a sphere.

gravity – the invisible force of attraction between objects.

light year – the distance travelled by light in a year (approximately 9.46 trillion km).

main sequence – the period of time when a star is carrying out nuclear fusion.

mass – the amount of material an object contains.

matter – physical things that exist in space as solids, liquids or gases.

nuclear fusion – the reactions that take place in the centre of the star that join the centre parts (nuclei) of atoms together, generating huge amounts of energy.

orbit – to travel around another object in space, in an elliptical path.

protostar – a star in the process of forming.

trillion – a million million.

FURTHER INFORMATION

Books

Space Travel Guides: The Sun and Stars
by Giles Sparrow (Franklin Watts, 2013)

The Earth and Space: The Sun
by Steve Parker (Wayland, 2009)

The World in Infographics: Space
by Jon Richards and Ed Simkins (Wayland, 2013)

Websites

http://www.esa.int/esaKIDSen/Starsandgalaxies.html
Information about stars and galaxies from the
European Space Agency.

http://www.cosmos4kids.com/files/stars_intro.html
Fun and clear explanations of how stars form, develop
and die, and the different types of galaxies.

http://www.lpi.usra.edu/education/skytellers/
galaxies/about.shtml
Pictures and facts about different types of galaxies.

INDEX